HOW MY BODY **WORKS**

Brain

Anita Ganeri

Evans Brothers Limited

First published by Evans Brothers Limited in 2006
2a Portman Mansions
Chiltern St
London W1U 6NR

British Library Cataloguing in Publication Data
Ganeri, Anita
Brain box
       1. Brain - Juvenile literature
       2. Human physiology - Juvenile literature
       I. Title
612.8'2

ISBN 0 237 53187 9
13-digit ISBN (from 1 January 2007) 978 0 237 53182 4

Credits

Editorial: Louise John
Design: Mark Holt & Big Blu Design
Artworks: Julian Baker
Consultant: Dr M Turner
Photographs: Steve Shott
Production: Jenny Mulvanny

Printed in China by WKT Co. Ltd

Acknowledgements
The author and publisher would like to thank the following for kind permission to reproduce photographs:

Science Photo Library, p.9 (Astid and Hanns-Frieder Michler), p.10 (Volker Steger), p.18 (CNRI), p.25 (BSIP, Laurent/Gluck), p.26 (Philippe Plailly); Richard Morgan, p.24.

Models from the Norrie Carr Agency and Truly Scrumptious Ltd. With thanks to: Imran Akhtar, Kaneesha Watt, Billy Hart, Michael Chin, Inaki Campbell-Arranz, Charlotte Hole, Jessica Ebsworth, Skye Johnson. Copyright © Evans Brothers Ltd 2003.

Contents

Brain power

Your brain is amazing. It is like a computer hidden inside your head. Your brain controls everything you do. It makes you think, learn and remember. It makes you feel things and makes sense of what is happening to you. It makes sure that every part of your body is working properly. Your body sends information to your brain. Then your brain sorts it out and tells your body what to do. Messages zoom around your body through long, thin wires, called **nerves**. Your brain and your nerves are called your nervous system.

AMAZING!

When you read a book, your eyes send messages to your brain about the words and pictures. Then your brain tells you what you are reading and seeing!

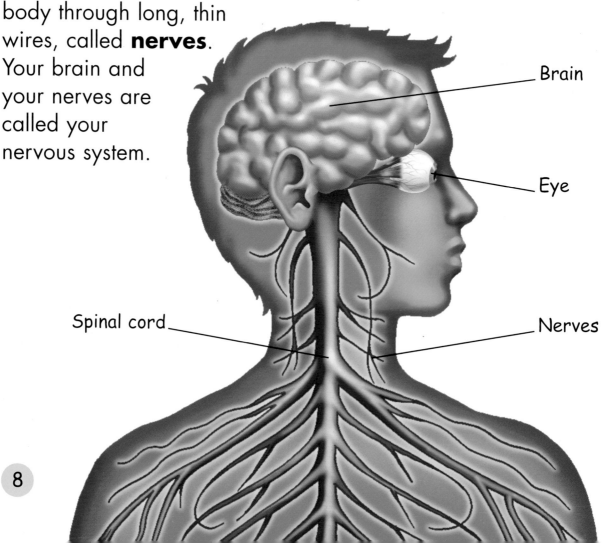

Brain

Eye

Spinal cord

Nerves

Your brain is the most important part of your body. Without it, your body wouldn't be able to work. Your brain sits inside a hard, bony case, called your **skull**. It protects your brain from bumps and knocks. The bones in your skull fit together like a jigsaw. This makes your skull very strong indeed.

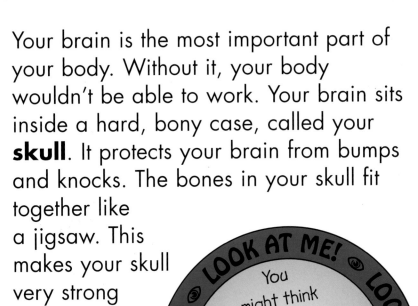

Your bony skull protects your delicate brain.

LOOK AT ME! You might think geniuses have big brains, but they don't. Everyone's brain is about the same size, however clever they are.

Your amazing brain

Your amazing brain fits snugly inside your skull, taking up the top half of your head. It looks a bit like a soft, wrinkly lump of wobbly, grey blancmange! An adult's brain weighs about 1.4 kilograms – that's about as much as six oranges.

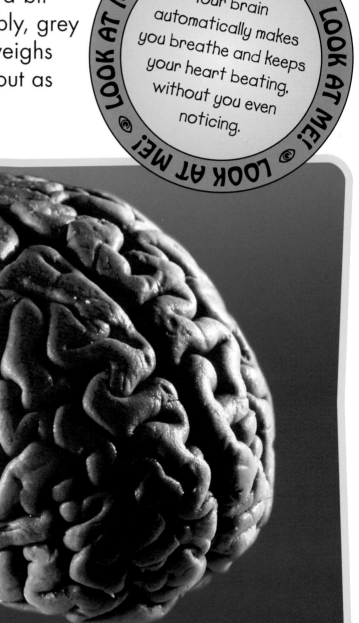

LOOK AT ME! LOOK AT ME! LOOK AT ME! LOOK AT ME! LOOK AT ME! LOOK AT ME!

Your brain automatically makes you breathe and keeps your heart beating, without you even noticing.

A human brain

Your brain is made from millions and millions of nerve **cells**. These are linked together for sending messages around your body. Each nerve cell is linked to thousands of others to make a vast nerve network. Your whole brain is covered in tiny tubes, called **blood vessels**. They carry **oxygen** from the air you breathe and goodness from the food you eat to your brain. Your busy brain needs lots of oxygen and food to keep it working properly. Around your brain is a tough skin that protects it from harm.

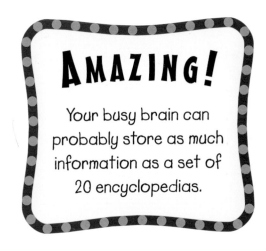

AMAZING!

Your busy brain can probably store as much information as a set of 20 encyclopedias.

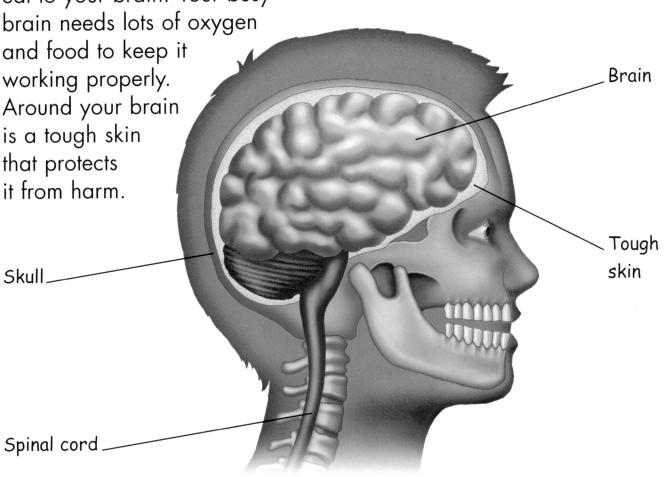

Brain

Tough skin

Skull

Spinal cord

Brain map

Your brain is divided into different parts. Each part sorts out different kinds of messages and has a different job to do. You can use the brain map shown here to find your way around.

SENSATION
This part gets messages from your skin.

SMELL
This part gets messages from your nose.

THALAMUS
This part makes you feel pain.

VISION
This part gets messages from your eyes.

HEARING
This part gets messages from your ears.

MOVEMENT
This part controls how you move.

MEMORY
These parts help you to remember and learn things.

LANGUAGE
This part makes you speak and lets you understand the words you read or hear.

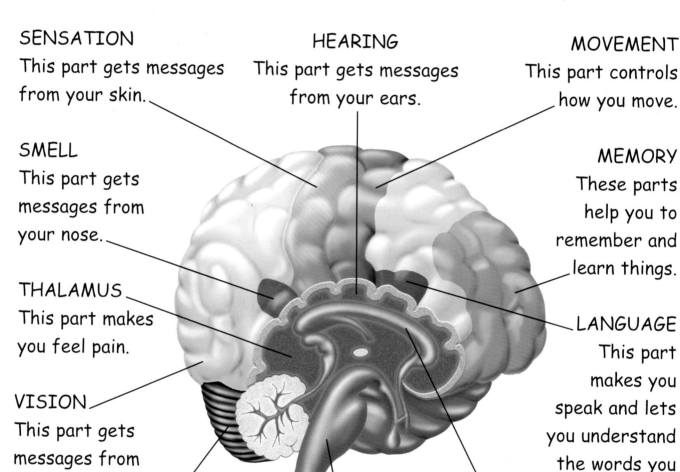

CEREBELLUM
This part helps you to balance and co-ordinate your movements. It stops you from falling over.

BRAIN STEM/MEDULLA
This part makes you breathe, swallow, cough and sneeze. It keeps your heart beating.

HYPOTHALAMUS
This part makes you feel hungry and thirsty. It also keeps your body at the right temperature.

LOOK AT ME! One part of your brain is in charge of only letting important messages through. Otherwise, your brain would soon get overloaded.

AMAZING!

Every day, thousands of your brain cells die and cannot be replaced. But don't worry - you've got lots and lots of them!

13

Left and right brain

The biggest part of your brain has two sides. The right side of your brain looks after the left side of your body. The left side of your brain looks after the right side of your body.

Each half of your brain looks after different skills and activities. In most people, the left side of the brain controls things that need careful thinking or working out, like doing sums or playing a game of chess. The right side of the brain controls artistic things, such as drawing, painting or playing a musical instrument.

AMAZING!

The two sides of your brain are joined together by a thick strap of more than 200 million nerves. They let messages pass from one side to the other.

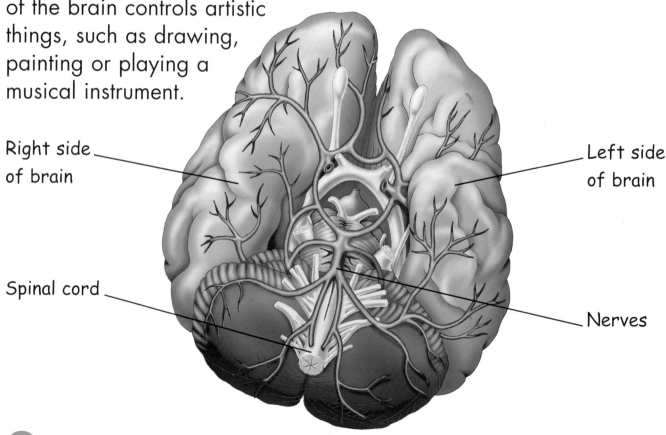

Right side of brain

Left side of brain

Spinal cord

Nerves

Are you left or right-handed? The hand you write with depends on which side of your brain controls your language and speaking. In right-handed people, the left side of the brain is in charge. In left-handed people, the right side is in charge. Very few people can write with both hands. They are called **ambidextrous**.

What a nerve!

Your nerves are like long, thin wires that run all around your body. They carry messages to and from your brain. If you have an itch, nerves in your skin send a message to your brain. Your brain notices the itch and sends a message back to your hand, telling it to scratch the itch.

LOOK AT ME! LOOK AT ME! LOOK AT ME! LOOK AT ME!

An itch can be caused by a bent-over hair in your skin.

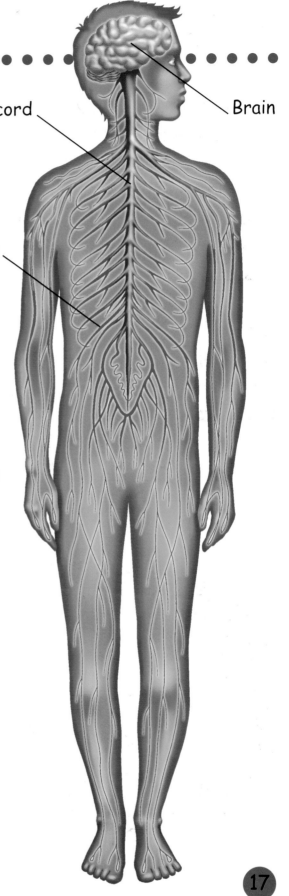

Spinal cord

Brain

Nerves

The main pathway for your nerves is down your back. A thick bundle of nerves, called your **spinal cord**, runs through your backbone. Messages from your brain travel down your spinal cord, then along nerves which branch out to every part of your body. Messages travel the other way from all over your body back up to your brain.

You have an amazing 100 million nerves in your body. Some carry messages from your five **senses** (your eyes, ears, nose, tongue and skin) to your brain. Some carry messages from your brain to your muscles. Some pass messages from one nerve to another.

How nerves work

Your nerves are made from bunches of nerve cells, which look like tiny wires. A nerve cell is so tiny that you need a **microscope** to see one, although some strings of nerve cells are more than a metre long. But how do your nerves work?

The nerve cells in your brain.

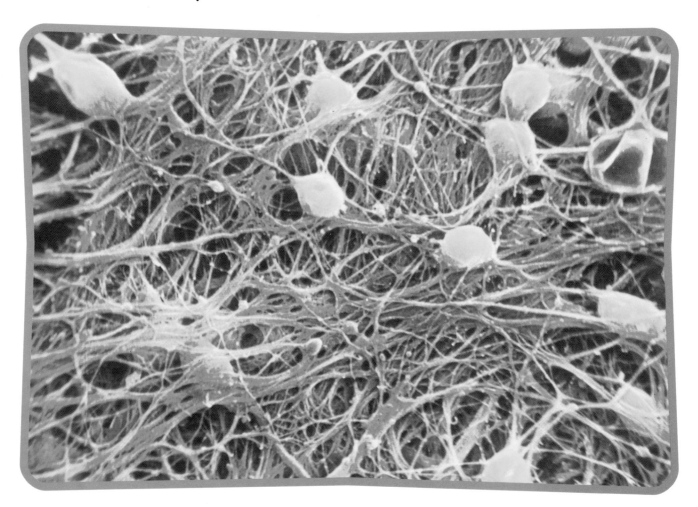

18

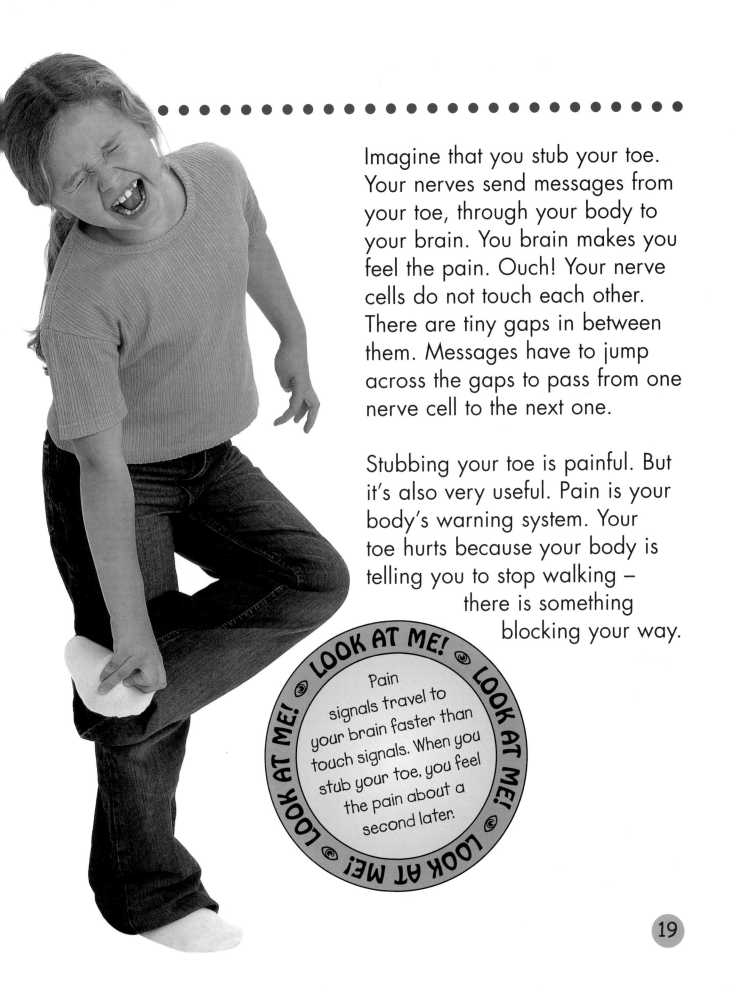

Imagine that you stub your toe. Your nerves send messages from your toe, through your body to your brain. You brain makes you feel the pain. Ouch! Your nerve cells do not touch each other. There are tiny gaps in between them. Messages have to jump across the gaps to pass from one nerve cell to the next one.

Stubbing your toe is painful. But it's also very useful. Pain is your body's warning system. Your toe hurts because your body is telling you to stop walking – there is something blocking your way.

LOOK AT ME! LOOK AT ME! LOOK AT ME! LOOK AT ME!

Pain signals travel to your brain faster than touch signals. When you stub your toe, you feel the pain about a second later.

Quick reactions

If you prick your finger on a pin, you snatch your hand away at once. You do not even think about it. This is called a **reflex action**. It helps to protect your body from danger. Usually, your nerves send a message to your brain. Then your brain sends a message to your muscles, telling them to move. In a reflex action, though, your nerves send a message straight to your muscles to tell them to move right away. This saves time.

LOOK AT ME! LOOK AT ME! LOOK AT ME! LOOK AT ME!

If you cross your legs and tap your knee gently just under your knee cap, does your leg jerk out? That shows your reflexes are working.

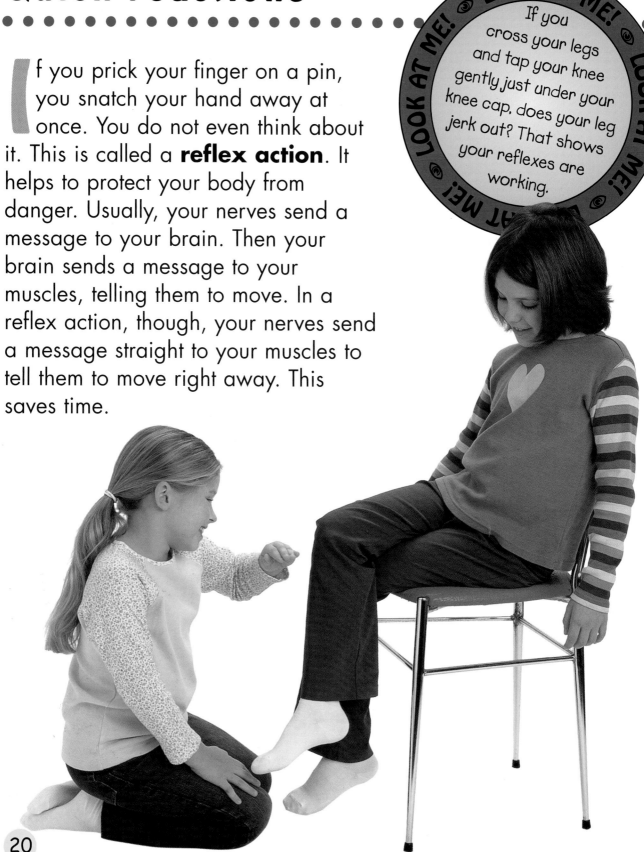

20

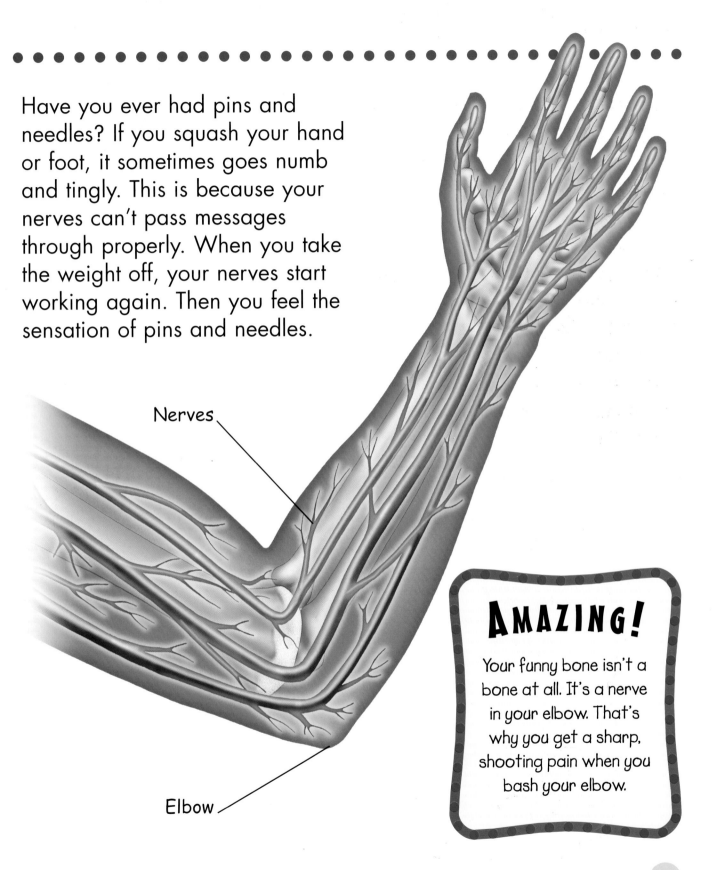

Have you ever had pins and needles? If you squash your hand or foot, it sometimes goes numb and tingly. This is because your nerves can't pass messages through properly. When you take the weight off, your nerves start working again. Then you feel the sensation of pins and needles.

Nerves

Elbow

AMAZING!

Your funny bone isn't a bone at all. It's a nerve in your elbow. That's why you get a sharp, shooting pain when you bash your elbow.

Learning a lesson

Your brain is also the part of your body that learns and remembers. You keep learning throughout your life. When you're a baby, you learn to smile, talk and walk. At school you learn to read and write.

Learning a lesson can be hard work. Take doing some sums, for example. Your teacher writes a sum on the blackboard. Your eyes look at it, then send information to your brain. Your brilliant brain works out the answer, then sends a message to your hand muscles to write it down.

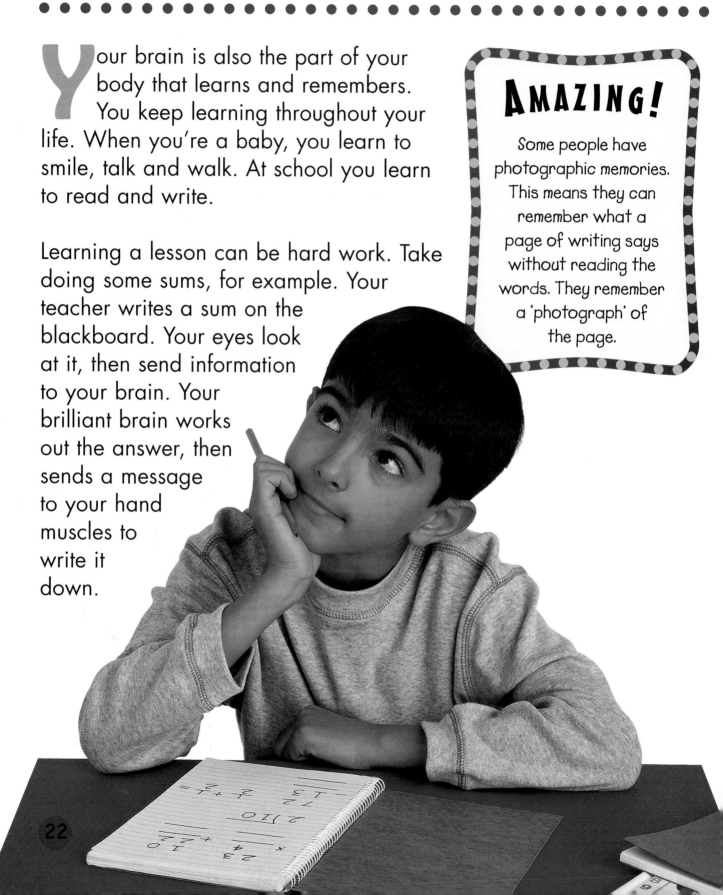

AMAZING!

Some people have photographic memories. This means they can remember what a page of writing says without reading the words. They remember a 'photograph' of the page.

22

As you learn, your brain stores information as **memories**. But your brain cannot remember everything. Otherwise it would run out of room. You remember important things, like your first day at school. But you forget little things, like what you had for tea last week.

LOOK AT ME! LOOK AT ME! LOOK AT ME! LOOK AT ME!

How good is your memory? Put ten objects on a tray. Look at them for 15 seconds, then look away. Try to remember as many objects as you can.

Good night!

Your brain and body work hard all day. Feeling tired is their way of telling you that they need to rest. When you're asleep, your body slows right down and your brain doesn't have to worry about what is happening all around you. But your brain doesn't stop working altogether. It makes sure that your heart keeps beating and that you keep breathing and **digesting** your food.

LOOK AT ME! ◎ LOOK AT ME! ◎ LOOK AT ME! ◎ LOOK AT ME! ◎

If you can't go to sleep, try a trick like counting sheep. How many sheep can you count before you drop off? One, two, three...

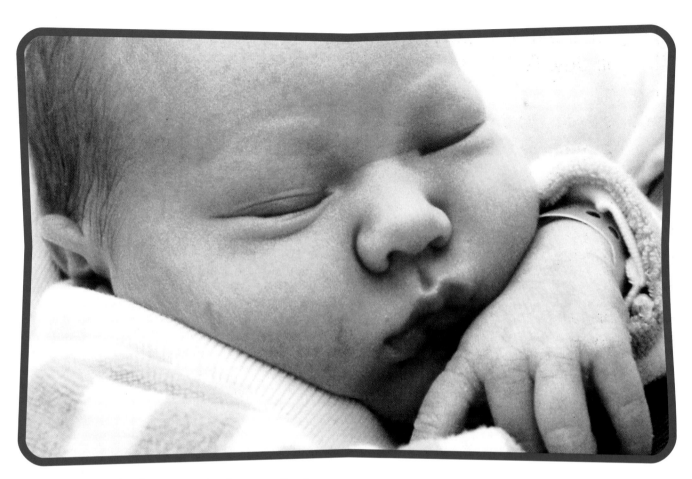

A newborn baby needs lots of sleep.

Sleep gives your body time to grow and mend itself. It also gives your brain a chance to sort out all the information it receives during the day. The amount of sleep you need depends on what you do during the day and how old you are. Adults need to sleep for about seven to eight hours a night and you probably need about ten hours' sleep a night.

AMAZING!

Newborn babies can sleep for up to an amazing 20 hours a day!

Sweet dreams

Dreams are stories or pictures your brain makes up while you are asleep. Even though they are not really happening, they feel very real. Dreams often have links with things that happen to you during the day. You might dream about a programme you watched on TV, or about something you read in a book. Some dreams are very strange and some dreams can be very scary. They are called **nightmares**. But don't worry – they stop when you wake up.

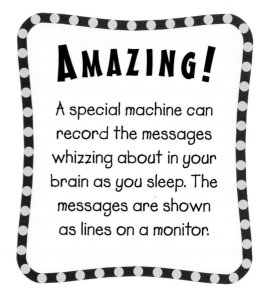

AMAZING!

A special machine can record the messages whizzing about in your brain as you sleep. The messages are shown as lines on a monitor.

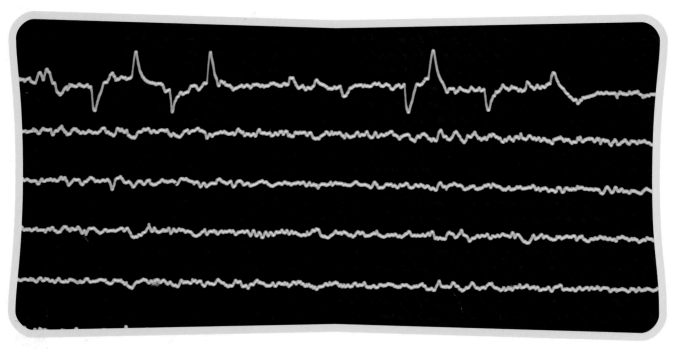

The jagged lines on the monitor show that your brain works hard even when you are asleep and dreaming.

There are lots of ideas about what dreams mean. If you dream you are flying, it might mean that you are feeling very happy or confident. If you dream you are falling, you might be worried about doing badly in a test or an exam at school. If you dream you are being chased, you might have a problem that needs to be solved.

LOOK AT ME! ⊚ LOOK AT ME! ⊚ LOOK AT ME! ⊚ LOOK AT ME!

Keep a pad and pencil by your bed and write down your dreams when you wake up in the morning, so that you can remember them.

Glossary

Ambidextrous Able to write just as well with the left or right hand.

Blood vessels The thin tubes which carry blood around your body.

Cells The tiny building blocks which make up every part of your body.

Digesting Breaking down your food into such tiny pieces that it can pass into your blood.

Memories Information about things that happened in the past, that you remember.

Microscope An instrument used for looking at objects which are too tiny to see otherwise.

Nerves Special cells which carry messages between your body and your brain. They look like thin wires.

Nightmares Bad dreams.

Oxygen A gas in the air which you need to breathe to stay alive.

Reflex action A reaction which happens automatically, such as snatching your hand away if you touch something very hot.

Senses The way in which your body tells you what is happening around you. Your five senses are hearing, touching, tasting, seeing and smelling.

Skull The hard case of bone in your head which protects your brain from knocks and bumps.

Spinal cord The bundle of nerves which runs down your back inside your spine (backbone).

Index